Hymns of My Soul

A Collection of Poetry by CoCheil

Literary Masterpiece Publishing | Ohio

Published in the United States by Literary Masterpiece Publishing

ISBN 10: 0-9974880-8-5

ISBN 13: 978-0-9974880-8-1

Printed in the United States of America
Ohio

Literary Masterpiece Publishing

5 stars

Reviewed By Vernita Naylor for Readers' Favorite

Do you enjoy poetry? What about artistic, visionary poetry? Picture this: over 75 poems of love, passion, rawness and connectivity from an artist's perspective; can you see it? As you begin to read Hymns of My Soul by CoCheil, you will discover a collection of poetry which takes the reader on a journey. These poems will allow the reader to witness the creative literary prowess of a master writer. In poems such as Sunrise and Sunset, In Love, Intense and Breathlessness, you can feel the various emotions that CoCheil wants the reader to feel through the words on the pages. The poems reach out and speak to you, whether you are sitting at the beach, at the library or in the comfort of your home. As you begin to read each poem, you will be able to feel and connect with each one.

I really enjoyed this set of poems because their beauty touched me in so many ways. Reading words in this book of vulnerability and intensity when expressing love of another and emotions such as "…but not as breath-taking as you…Seeing you today made me feel some type of way" or "No emotion I can hide, and if I trust you, I will let you inside" depicts the love in essence of rhythm or rhyme that CoCheil expresses so masterfully. I loved how the words put my mind in sync with the visions portrayed within the words of the poems. If you're looking for some hope in the form of art, add this book to your library.

"Art enables us to find ourselves and lose ourselves
at the same time" – Thomas Merton

<u>Illogical</u>

Fluid...
My veracity like a parallel universe unseen yet is
there
Like a place of forbidden nevermind only decoded in
the unconscious mind
Too complex for the faint hearted yet too simple for
the simple
A paradox...
Senselessness like a type of illogicality
A word I created representing the trangression of
the rules of logic
Opposites like the ying yang yet no balance is
maintained
Fluid...
Everything's distorted so meanings are seemingly
meaningless
All seems mundane, insignificant, and borderline
ignorable
The heart is no longer red; it's blue like the hue the
moon illumes against the snow in the winter
A paradox...
My veracity as I succomb to the illogicality of a
seemingly parallel universe not wanting to go red...

<u>My Heart Sings</u>

My heart sings a tune not many can understand
Flying free like a bird yet preparing to land
My soul; everything about me is nothing more than
art
Upon meeting me, could you hear the melody of my
heart?
An excellent conversationalist yet a FAR better
writer
Sensitive yet not weak; I'm a warrior, survivor, and
fighter
I can comb through all of the cellular follicles of you
I'm so tired of the ignorance; what that mouth do?
Explore me like I'm a treasure map
Stop assuming and explore me…perhaps?
I'm not what you're used to and this is not arrogance
speaking
It's the fact that not too many are reaching the way
that I'm reaching
Looking towards the stars…
…because…
…My fantastical mind thinks I should be where they
are
Fuck money, I want to leave a legacy
Long after my death, through my work folks will
remember me…
…especially my favorite girl
I will drown you; only the strong can handle the
depths of my world

I'll let you breathe just don't cage me
Let me fly free
My heart sings a tune not many can understand
I'll keep flying because a part of me is not ready to
land

Forbidden Love

Thunderous clouds linger like nightmares fraught
and foil

Trying to suppress the sunset; diffuse the glow for
happiness' spoil

A sigh pampered across time at hence

Blights of rhyme and reason bright as future's tense

Spent to cosset for care to cease as all seems weary

Like a treasure; true thoughts and ideals forbiddenly
buried

As a breeze touches the face as the hand of God

Heed the concern as fraught is odd

Out of place, no pace, no face, for feelings succumb

Present tense of disillusion as there's no place to run

Thunderous clouds linger like nightmares fraught
and foil

The sunset shines through the darkness embraced by
seeds planted in happiness' soil…

The Masterpiece

Art; whispers to the soul a language only translatable
to the heart
A proposition to paint you; without the colors to
start
Representative of personality and poise: a direction
Which medium was proper; an endearing question
Intrigue and mystery, a quiet sexiness that thoughts
provoke
Like a beautiful painting, intense emotions and
desires evoked
Envisioning the painting in my dreams, but my
hands unworthy to touch the surface
This masterpiece; I wanted a master's piece as
visions of mistakes made me nervous
Could I ruin it all from rushing one stroke of my
brush?
Could I ruin it all from relinquishing the color of my
touch?
All imperfections perfectly perfect in the eyes of this
beholder

Subjective to most, but to the artist, a piece that outdoes the skills of its sculptor

Falling in love with the work that basically unfolded itself

Putting my name on a piece these hands never felt

Bright colors, earth tones, or monotones, which are reflective of you?

You're a mixed media work; one medium could never capture the complete essence of you

A painting that came into existence practically on its own

A work of art I'm proud of and want admired by the young and old

Art; whispers to the soul a language only translatable to the heart

By trying to paint you, you transformed me into your latest work of art…

Drown You

I want to drown you…
I want to submerse you into the sea of me
Even under water, you'll still be able to breathe
I desire to be your everything
Bless you with every facet of what true love brings
I want you to feel at peace when we commingle
Anytime you think of me, I want your soul to tingle
Feel me…
…Just feel me…
Put your hands, heart, and soul all over me
Tickle me with the sound of your laugh
Let me into the dark places to show you a light you
never knew you had
I want you to feel my touch even when you're away
Just let me hold you even if you don't have any
words to say
There is nothing I would ever deny you
All I ask is that you don't hide you…
…from me
We can discuss anything no matter how ugly
I want to be your sunrise in the morning and your
sunset before night
I'd rather love on you than to fight
Let me be your star
My love can heal any of your scars
Trust in me
Promise to never cage me
Let me bless you with what true love brings
Let me be your everything

I want to submerse you into the sea of me
Even under water, you'll still be able to breathe
Let me drown you

<u>Time and Space</u>

Voices echo as silent cries 'tis sense…

Alas the resonance of forevermore at resilience bent

A luxury yet curse unaffordable to most

Life's incubator; an invisible womb silently

whispering like a ghost

Tis endless times amount to a moment's grace

Almost infinite in the mind outside the realm of time

and space

A sigh representative of a pause in time…

Frozen still an illusion that deceived thine mind…

Yet the fantasy felt so real; breathlessness

As it was imagined, a love beyond heaven sent

Dissipated like the deep fog in early spring…

A halo envisage as the heart impulsively crowned thy

queen

Aloof; surrendered to a forbidden spell

That rests only in the mind as the soul awaits to

exhale…

A fallacy only spoken amongst the midst

A reality if a Genie could grant one wish

'Tis endless times amount to a moment's grace…

A treasure of the mind as envisioned in a moment of

time and space…

<u>My Heart Sees</u>

Blindness...
I can close my eyes...
But my heart still sees
I can close my mind...
But my heart still sees...
I can close my ears...
But my heart still sees
I can turn my back...
But my heart still sees
My heart is like a wild animal that not even I can
tame
Trying to get my mind to override my heart feels like
with myself I'm playing a dangerous game
Feelings flowing deeper than the deepest trench
drowning me as I'm prevented from reaching the
surface...
So I can breathe...
The thought or possibility of being hurt doesn't even
make me nervous...
A repetitive seed...
That I plant yet nothing grows
I'm blind to repercussions even if my mind knows
Blindness...
I can close my eyes...
But my heart sees

I can close my mind...
But my heart sees
I can close my ears...
But my heart sees
I can turn my back...
But my heart sees
Drowning me in the deepest trenches of my own
emotions
Unable to breathe or to focus
Trying to escape by using my mind
Although my heart sees...
...she remains blind

<u>Justice</u>

Justice…
What does that truly mean?
For folks whose hearts have seen…
…so much pain…
The type that drains…
…the soul…
Yearning to know the reason why
As we shed 'silent' tears trying to swallow our pride
Again…
Hurt as fuck yet trying to pretend…
…that all is well
Because we have to ensure that everyone else is well
Where does that strength begin?…
…maybe I'm not as strong as God thinks I am and
resend…
Implode in a sense…
However?…
Unexplainable events are in Heaven's tense…
God does what he does and it's not to leave us
bent…
…out of shape…
…out of place…
His purpose is to show us the light…
…heal us from the darkness and help us realize the
meaning of our plight…
…it's not in vain…
…I completely understand your pain…
…on a different plane…

The 'stinch' of death sometimes haunts me…
…even though I'm often down on bended knee
Looking towards the skies for God…
…seeing him through his creations from afar which
may sound odd…
Your heart may feel a bit 'tangled'
But?...
…you now personally know the name of your new
Guardian Angel…
Justice?...
What does it truly mean?
When behind the scenes?...
…your soul screams…

<u>Hurt</u>

Distorted reflection from the rain stained window…
Staring at my eyes as the droplets drizzle down the
glass as the wind blows
Sounds violent, gusty as though a storm is coming
An illusion, because the trees barely bend like a hint
of peace is being summoned
Staring intensely at the grey skies reminiscent of my
mood
Attempting to keep my mind busy, searching for
something to soothe…
…the pain that I hide deep down inside of me…
Love can set you free but it can also make you feel
like you can't breathe…
No air…
No air…
Trying to move on but it doesn't seem to go
anywhere…
Like I'm being held captive against my will
Wishing I could turn my emotions off and not
feel…
…a thing…
Just be numb inside
But from my heart I cannot hide…
Staring at my eyes as they reflect against the rain
stained glass…
My reflection is smiling but my eyes look so sad
My reflection is crying tears my pride won't allow to
escape the back of my eyes
Silently, my soul continuously cries…

Attempting to keep my mind busy, searching for something to soothe…
…wondering how my soul can heal from this bruise…
Staring intensely at the grey skies yearning for a rainbow
…as droplets drizzle down the glass as the wind blows
Distorted reflection from the rain stained window…
My eyes match my reflection as tears flow…
No air…
No air…
I can't breathe…

Missing You

The stroke of my brush, a masterpiece I forbade

Echoing sounds of water splattering against the

window pane

Insanely driven into a state of solitude

Bright colors fill the canvas attempting to establish

the mood

Of gestures, reminiscent of how minds silently

converse

Like a magnet, souls actually thirst

For a sentence, one mention, so unduly true

The soul speaks through the canvas, a power, even

words cannot do

The stroke of my brush, a masterpiece that takes

days

Echoing the sounds of my soul as sunlight beams

through the window pane…

<u>Love</u>

From a moment's passing, sprinkled onto my heart
like morning dew
It's difficult to fathom how quickly I've fallen for
you
Like I'm under a spell without an antidote.
I feel like I can stand in the rain without getting
soaked
Your words mesmerize and intrigue as my hands
paint your soul
Your presence has me telling stories left untold
Many of nights, I desperately tried to shake what I
feel
Terrified; could this be real?
So intensely passionate; it runs so deep
Breathlessness as I see your face in my sleep
To runaway?
I did, but I have to let this be
Only through love are we truly set free

<u>Can't Let Go; Forevermore</u>

Rantings of a drunken whore

Beating at my chamber door

My mind says, "Go away",

But my heart simply can't ignore

I implore then open the door

To a tear stained face and a silent cry

No matter what she did, I can't take the look of pain

in her eyes

Her soul is cracked as I wonder who did it

As emotionally drained as I am, I have to help her

fix it

I know she can't do it on her own

Like a sponge, I absorb her emotions, and it's so

strong

Sucking and sucking that pain out of her into me

Needing extra sleep 'cause it's literally draining me,

But I can't let go

I can't turn anyone away

I'm obsessed with the word "save"

Rantings of a drunken whore

Beating at my chamber door

My mind says, "Go away",

But my heart simply can't ignore

This heart of mine is my curse…

Forevermore.

Goodbye Love

That sparkle in the eyes that glisten like stars
sprinkled against the black canvas of the night sky
like gemstones.
The sound of that voice as beautiful as the melody
of rushing waters echo in my ears when alone
That smile that is reminiscent of the bright glow
from the sun; almost too beautiful to behold
A soul that is similar to, but is different, from yet
speaks the same melody as my soul
An unexplainable balance of two hearts and two
minds
One passive, one aggressive but like the ying-yang
they bind
A balancing act creating a distance at hence
A connection that is both past yet present tense
An unforgettable-ness that both dismiss in time
Suspended within different eras, wants and needs,
ideals, and rhyme
We silently speak to each other; a call we can feel
within our thoughts

Although everything we had, thought we had,

actually didn't have, is lost

Within the realm of time and space floated away like

a cold front

Torrential rains, crashing lightning, even sunny days

as confusion on both sides rest at the forefront.

Some things are unexplainable, sometimes

inconceivable, but sometimes the thing to do is

often left unspoken

You spoke a language only my soul could transcribe

more potent than your average love potion

Everything, including the mundane, happens for a

reason even if the reason doesn't make sense

Nothing lasts forever, so we must cherish everything

for the short space that it's sent

Sometimes the most difficult yet stupidest thing to

do is walk away and say goodbye

But you leave when your heart wanted you to stay

due to not trusting how you feel, stubbornness, and

pride

You would give anything for another chance to be
hypnotized by those almond-shaped dark brown
eyes
Trying to shake off what you feel because the
distance is burning you inside
That sparkle in the eyes that glisten like stars
sprinkled against the black canvas of the night sky
like gemstones
Will forever stain my heart, intrigue my mind,
playing a melody on repeat to my soul, imprinted in
my memory every night my eyes close.

<u>Falling in Love</u>

Feeling the warmth of the sun massaging my cheek
on a rainy day

Hearing birds chirping harmoniously on a bitterly
cold winter day

Feeling cool breezes molest my body during the
desert's heat wave

Hearing nature sounds like a beautiful symphony
that goes on for days

Feeling your touch from a simple thought

Hearing your voice in my head brightening my day
in ways I never thought

Feeling near you although you're far away and can't
be next to me

Hearing the song of your heart and loving the
melody

Feel…

Hear…

Feel…

Hear…

Seeing the invisible silhouette of

Hearing the silent voice of

Feeling the illusory touch of…

…falling in love…

<u>Finding herself Again</u>

Rain forcibly smacking against the window pane

Lightning striking the earth igniting flames

Thunder roaring loudly across the skies

Reminiscent of the pain in the back of a woman's

eyes

Waterfalls calmly crashing down

The peaceful wilderness, like music, full of sounds

Beautiful flowers bloom symbolic of birth

Reminiscent of a woman realizing her worth

Boulders crashing down as the mountain moves

The tears of angels quietly soothe

Volcanoes erupt with energy as lava poureth

Reminiscent of a woman that restored her courage

Stars glisten in the night speaking volumes

The moon smiles at mother earth as her magnet calls

him

The clouds show the beginning and the end

Reminiscent of a woman dreaming again.

Sunlight reflecting across the open seas

Seeing the rhythmic laughter of the leaves on the

trees

Tropical winds caressing the body so gracefully one

can't get enough

Reminiscent of a woman in love…

The World Wasn't Grand Enough

The world wasn't grand enough
For the plans God had for you
Secretly wondering the things HE may have said to you
Your heart was too pure for a world like this
And no matter how much we miss you,
You live through your kids
Although you're his little brother,
I've always viewed you as my dad's twin
And you both battled the same sin
Then overcame
To lose you so unexpectedly and so soon is a shame
But is it really?
Or could it be a wake-up call for us to get on our knees and look towards the ceiling?
In the valley of our emotions, needing internal healing
But God knows what's he's doing and will never leave us reeling
Even during the storms, your heart couldn't be dismissed
And you will forever be loved and missed
The world just wasn't grand enough
Every tear shed shows how much you are loved
You are in a much better place
Please let Grover know that I miss the sound of his voice and seeing his face
The world just wasn't grand enough…

...for the plans God has for the ones he loves...

Whisper

Whisper…
Only a select few can hear
And in order to hear?
She has to let you near
She's not one to allow many to get close to her
If she lets you in, you are special to her
It doesn't always have to be in a romantic sense
Sometimes, a woman just needs a friend
And other times?
She gets so used to solitude that she doesn't know
how to reach
She often says more with her facial expressions than
with her speech
She writes better than she speaks
She doesn't say much because her actions speak
Volumes…
Of her true character if one takes notice
An odd one…
When stressed or overwhelmed, she's more focused
Withdraws into herself and finds peace in her work
Can be mean as f*ck yet quick to give a homeless
person her shirt
A walking paradox that moves to the beat of her
own drum
A woman that believes by simply trying you've
already won
There's a silent "power" within her presence
And always willing to accept life as it comes; learning
all the lessons

And sharing her experiences with a select few
And she means it from the depths of her soul
whenever she says, "I love you"
Caring too much is her Achilles heel
However, she's unafraid to speak what her heart
feels
An intensity that's unmatched…
As disappointments make her desire to detach
But even if she unplugs her heart, the fire doesn't
exhaust
No matter what she feels, she will leave a toxic
situation like a boss
Whisper…
Only a select few can hear
And in order to hear?
She has to allow you to come near
She's not one to allow many to get close to her
 For the first time in her life, she fears getting hurt…

<u>In Love</u>

Love…
There's so many ways…
Platonic, unconditional, friendship, romantic, and
more
Sooooo many days…
A deep emotion that eludes some folks because
they're afraid…
…to implore
Yet, folks yearn for the definition there of
Have to take a breather…
Because…
..it touches us in such a special way
When eyes can say much more than words could
ever say…
…listen…
…just listen…
…nothing is like when those eyes glisten…
When they're glad to see another
…and their hearts and souls bind with another
Written across the stars
A blessing those feelings are…
Love…
There's so many ways…
Platonic, unconditional, friendship, romantic, and
the others more
Romantic love will have me knocking at your
chamber door
Wanting you; yearning for you and only you
Relinquishing my soul making you my morning dew

But?
You're not hearing me…
…a part of me thinking that you may feel me…
You're not used to a love deeper than the Marinara trench
Something that will have you drenched…
…may even "drown" you…
In a definition of love that you've never knew
Love…
Soooo many days…
There's so many ways…
Platonic, unconditional, friendship, romantic, and more
But this heaven sent blessing will always remain…
Just let me in your chamber door…

The Dancer

The dancer…
The rhythm and tone
Touches one straight to the bone
Something seemingly magical one may want to hone
Through the mind feeling like one can fly like a
drone
That dancer…
With that gracefulness
A "complicated" poetry in motion one can't forget
A beautiful symmetry that's greater than less
Dancing the heart of your soul; a gorgeous mess
The dancer…
…Is poetry in physical motion
Body movements often says more than most words
spoken
The movements are like a potion
Admirable by any intelligence quotient
The dancer…
Speaks silently to the soul
And gives a hell of a show
Body moves in ways only the soul knows
And through the performance, their hearts show
That dancer…
…the dancer…
Speaks without saying a word…
…yet touches many…

Wounded Soldier

Wounded soldier

Keep your head held high

It's not a sign of weakness; it's okay to cry

Holding emotions inside will lead you to an early

grave

Time heals all wounds starting today

Stop holding onto memories of a daunting past

The pain in your heart will not last

Patch yourself up for those wounds will heal

Pick yourself up and get back out on that field.

Wounded soldier

Keep your head held high

All wounds heal; don't let the fire burn out of your

eyes…

So Long

So long, so long,

Is in the song

And in the way you're gone

So far yet near

Giving me courage yet fear

Causing such pain yet erasing tears

Memories of a past that's also present

Both dreadful yet pleasant

A smile reminiscent of heaven

Sigh

Making me smile yet sigh

Causing me to realize

Sometimes it's best to deny

So long, so long

Is in the song

And in the way you're gone

But I will remain strong

<u>Can I Paint You?</u>

Can I paint you?...
Not your external beauty, but what I see inside of
your soul
Can I tell you what I see in the back of your eyes
when you "play" like your heart is cold?
Can I write you?...
A new story that accentuates every single positive
attribute
Can I hand you a mirror so you can see the beauty
that lies within you?
Can I photograph you?...
Capture those special yet simple joyous moments
you think people don't see
Can I heal the wounds that silently bleed?
Can I frame you?...
I want you to fly free like a bird as I inspiringly
watch you
And think to myself, "There goes my boo."
Can I climb any mountains with you?...
And erase every bit of fear that may be within you
I have no harmful intent; just wanna uplift you
Can I sculpt you?...
Your essence, your presence is what I would like to
pursue
Can I have a simple glimpse inside of you?
Can I paint you?...
Just let me paint you
I want the colors of my love all over you

<u>The Rose; Thorns and Thistles</u>

Every rose has its thorns,

    but every thorn is not the only latch on the

stem of that rose

        …thorns & thistles…

The prickles of the thistle;

    more painful than thorns…

        …grown wild; untamed…

Concealing secrets…

    therein contains the likeness of fruit

        …delicious; vulnerable…

The thistle is armor

    …grows slowly…

A hassle to get through the prickles to the fruit…

Some people appear to be simple roses…

    …beautiful…

A compliment to anyone's garden…

    …a must have…

        …challenging upkeep…

    …captivates…

    With thorns attached to their stems…

The admirer dismounts each thorn…

…one by one…

Perceiving the rose as safe…

…prepared to mount in the garden…

A masterpiece…

Pampering and giving it care to keep it bloomed…

…beautiful…

In the center of that beautiful rose…

…lies a thistle…

The prickles of the thistle are painful…

…yet…

…one by one…

…removing…

…hurts then heals…

…hurts then heals…

Making you wonder…

Why did I desire that rose in the first place?…

…sigh…

You've come too far…

…one by one…

…removing…

That glimpse of beauty within…

Your burning desire motivates…

 …hurting and healing…

  …hurting and healing…

 …that glimpse…

   …that ideal…

That beauty you must…

 …sigh…

You have to call your own…

 …removing…

  …one by one…

 …hurting and healing…

  …hurting and healing…

 …sigh…

You've dismounted every single prickle…

 …accomplished…

  …your prize…

 You deserve it…

The fruit appears delicious; loving…

 A fairy tale…

  …a must have…

…sigh…

Impatient to try…

…disappointed…

…bitter sweet…

Isn't fruit after all…

…another thistle…

Your eyes have deceived your senses,

as you removed the thorns & thistles…

they latched onto you…

…the self-deceit…

The rose failed you…

Transformed you into a thistle with thorns along your stem;

Mounted the soil with your prized rose…

Refusing to rid the ideal…

Ruining your own garden…

Your desired rose dismounted you in the process…

…thorns & thistles…

…removing…

In search of fruit that does not exist…

…hurts then heals…

...hurts then heals...

...a continuous cycle...

The garden quickly barrens...

Nothing grows...

Fertile soil;

the love essential to growth...

...none is left...

Only thorns & thistles...

...of two souls afraid to give up...

In loyal...

Not love...

To uproot?...

...it's better...

Less is more...

More is less...

Piercing the carnation...

The one you bypassed for the beauty of the rose...

...sigh...

In full bloom...

...sigh...

In full splendor...

...sigh...

More beautiful now than it's ever been...

...sigh...

Realizing...

You should have complemented your garden with
the carnation...

...roses?...

...SIGH!...

...thorns and thistles...

...hurts then heals...

Constantly removing...

Until the soil...

...becomes desolate.

You Take Away

You take away…
Not only my breath, my light, my shine
Wanting to mend your heart with the love that's
within mine
Pause…
…to no avail
Misery and pain is what your essence expels
But what am I to do?
With this compassionate soul that loves and wants to
heal you
But how can I?
…when all I mainly see is a lunar eclipse in the back
of your eyes…
Your smile shines brightly, but it's feigned
Wanting to dance with you in the rain
For I've seen how cold this world can be
Can I pump your heart with every breath you
breathe?
…to no avail
I just wish you'll allow me to delve…
…into everything about you that you try to conceal
Talk to me…
Let me into how you truly feel
I see you, and you're like poison to my brain
For some reason, your imprint is in my heart stained
You hurt me, I hurt you; a cycle that ceases to end
Turn around and state, "I need you my friend"
I absorb and absorb as you take and take
My heart is exhausted needing a break

...to no avail
We're better off by ourselves
I've let you go, but will you let me?
My love no longer hangs on my sleeve
You're hanging onto a dream that never truly existed
And from my heart, you've been evicted
You take away...
...you take away...
...and I've retired my cape...

Reminiscence

Reminiscence…

Visions that creep in at night

Opposite the room, the sun lights

The darkest creases of souls

To behold…

To consume…

To be consumed

By hearts with closed rooms

No way in, peering through a crack

Seeing a set of eyes that momentarily wink back

Hollowed from inside out

From a stare, as silence is a shout

The heart speaks

As the words, echo away out of reach

But visions still creep in at night

Opposite the room, the sun lights

The silhouette of a glimpse of love…

…Reminiscence

Orgasm

A power surge of energy through the gentle gliding of flesh

An indescribable presence fluttering throughout the essence

An intensity of passion unto the spiritual in scenes

Frame by frame; inch by inch

Passion so deeply imbedded yet freed from the soul

Intensity as rhythms in motion

An orchestra only heard by two

Chirping along into one dance

A breeze that tingles down the body in waves

Rippling the warmth in tense

Intensity as rhythms in motion

Frame by frame; inch by inch

An indescribable presence rippling throughout the essence

Until it's released…

Speechless

Speechless…
I wanna be down with your groove
The way you move…
My soul…
Difficult for me to maintain and control…
You play like a movie in my head when you're not near
When I look into your eyes, your soul is clear
Yearning…
Yet still learning…
Each other…
Taking my time; not trying to smother
…you…
That gleam in your eyes, and the p*ssy is as wet as morning dew
A drunken statement perhaps…
…I just know I want to make you bend your back…
…in complete ecstasy…
Wanting you to want me and only me
I guess that's an elaborate dream though
Let me suck it nice and slow...
Your love faces don't be afraid to show
After this, I doubt if you consider me as a platonic friend
I wanna see how those legs bend
Speechless…
I wanna be down with your groove…
Thank me in the morning by the way I make that body move

<u>Breeze</u>

A breeze…

Like a summer's passing through the hollows of time

Whispering ambiguities as intangible as a reason

The heat of the flame feeling twice removed

Surrendered…

It surrendered; we surrendered…

The fantasy for a veracity too unfeigned for the
imagined

Fluid; like the sounds heard when submerged
underwater

Gasping for air although we're already above the
surface

Once ignited flames within from a simple glance

Torching the sheets with our rhymes and rhythms

Inexplicable how the storm clouds emerged

Removing the heat and dousing the flame

Burned out; it burnt out…

Leaving smoldering coals willing to reignite in
present or future tense

The winter never felt colder

Remembering the summer before its passing

The air was so crisp to inhale

The warmth from the sun penetrated my essence

Sigh; I sighed…

My heart skipped a beat as my soul smiled

Whispering ambiguities as intangible as a song

Like a winter's passing through the hollows of time

The breeze?...

…I still feel it…

Forbidden Dance

The forbidden dance…

Like a motion that lacks emotion; pure animal instinct

The id meeting conscious awareness without any control

Pure adrenaline matching the mental vision

Hot flashes from hidden burning desires

Needing a cold shower but even that can't tame the body

The mind has locked its target like a missile launcher

Wanting to give your body contorted schisms for the rhythms as we lock eyes

Wanting to connect your soul with mine; for the moment

Let me be the blues in your thighs as we take this thing to spiritual heights

Lust, lust, and more lust; making the mouth salivate

Wanting to make your body tingle every time you think of me

Wanting to make you shiver as your lips quiver and
you're left speechless
Nothing but tears drizzling down your face as we
embrace
The forbidden dance…

Listen

Listen…

To sounds that seem inaudible

Closed-caption without caption though speaks to the

soul

An unconscious level of understanding as emotions

evoke

Silence…silence…

Listening to the rhythm of one's heart

Like seeing a portion of a rainbow not knowing if

that point is the end or the start

A seemingly magical covenant no one agreed yet

leaves its mark

Listen…

As the eyes close in an unnoticeable sigh

Using your hands to create visual poetry that speaks

words folks can't deny

Emotions flowing deeper than a black hole being

expressed as you prepare to fly

Silence…silence…

A beautiful thing for those that think deeply

Inaudible melodies that almost romantically sing to

me

Like an inexplicable connection to God that beeches

me

Listen…

Just listen…

Art speaks the language of my soul…

…if you just listen…

From Hello

You had me at "Hello"…
That long gaze we gave pierced my soul
Didn't know you at the time, yet chills went through
my spine
That natural external beauty seemed to stop time…
…at least through my eyes
Wondering the secrets that may have lied behind
those eyes
A little secret I must confess…
My walls were unto the heavens, but you were up for
the test
It was a lot to crack open my chest
Although…
…You had me at "Hello"…
I was open yet reclusive to relinquish my soul
You've stargazed with me
Did you find those things that give me peace
interesting?
Did I bore you?…
…by the methods in which I desired to explore you?
There is much more to me than I am willing to show
My process of unraveling my inner self is slow
If you would've been patient, I would've been
patient
Trust, love is pure to me; I could never fake it
You had me at "Hello"
Unfortunately, you wanted something I couldn't give
you

You thought the sky was purple, yet I saw it as
blue…
　…And all the colors of the sunrise and sunset
Too very different I guess…
…had me soaking the pillows in tears and not sweat
Things happen for a reason
And I'm proud to say that I've been switched
seasons
Contacting me due to your regret
I'm someone you realize after all of these years you
should have kept
You once had me at "Hello"
But?...
I've evicted you from my soul
Sometimes the best thing to do is to let it go
I want someone that notices the sky is blue yet pays
attention to the different hues
And will show me the rainbow of their soul as well
as allow me to be their morning dew
Sprinkle you…
…sprinkle you…
…with the positive images I see in you…
"Hello"…
"Hello"…
Some folk's had me at "Hello"…
…I once put my cape on to try to heal their souls…
…but now?...
I'm the one that needs a healing soul

Sunrise and Sunset

Sunrise and sunset; both beautiful yet mysterious in
its origins from fresh eyes of breathless beauty
Ruled by Venus the goddess of love; to genuinely
care is your duty
You perceive the world through the eyes of a gifted
child; noticing the love throughout any pain
Silently inspiring the world around you with nothing
needed in return; smiles and gratitude are what you
are to gain.
Life is so short, precious, and beautiful; a concept
you seem to grasp better than most
You can literally feel the breeze in your soul living
and enjoying life at the highest dose
Your mystery, beauty, strength, and beyond
mesmerizes even the cruelest soul
When you love, you genuinely love, and love hard
making it difficult to let go

You're optimistic and positive; a true blessing that lights the dark corners of everyone's soul, but I know you're hurting inside.

A beautiful mind and beautiful face without a big name; smiling with your eyes and positive spirit to conceal what's really going on inside.

You've lost two angels; yet you've gain two more guardians to keep you safe

I wish I could be there to hold you, console you, and wipe away any tear that may drizzle down your face

The one's you love left a cruel chaotic world for an unimaginable peace; a much better place.

This is not a goodbye; it's an "until we meet again" – one day again you will see their face.

Sunrise and sunset; both beautiful yet mysterious in its origins representative of a new beginning and a new life

You're a strong woman and can take care of yourself, but even at a distance, I'm always here by your side…

I'm praying for you and your family…

Fire

Fire's ablaze, burning within the core; the purest of light

From old coals that's never been ignited; didn't know they could ignite

Illuminating a small corner of my soul

Didn't want to fall in love, so I battled myself losing my self-control

Insignificant to most; magnificent to the host

Trying to extinguish my own flame; choking off my own smoke

"Shake it off, you've gotta shake it off" my inner voice silently screamed

Insignificant; I convinced myself to believe

That I was not an empty shell longing to be filled

Secrets locked away for years would not be spilled

I don't want something that can tangibly be felt; setting me free from the prison of me

But I was self-deceived

From the moment we spoke, I knew it was meant to
be

Moving slowly, carefully, wanting feelings to grow
naturally

Shattered heart that reflected a terrible choice

Glued back together by kind words and the sound of
a voice

That voice that rings in my ears unto this very day

That voice that has me unable to sleep for days

That voice that ignited my soul

That voice that I let go

Fire's ablaze, burning within my core; so out of my
sight

From old coals that's never been ignited; felt weird
for them to ignite

Illuminating a facet of my life

Torching my soul as I hear that voice echo in my
ears at night

Reminding me of how I returned to the prison of
me; my comfort zone

Burning my own heart as the flames blaze on...

<u>Open My Eyes</u>

Open my eyes?...
How about you allow me to open yours and explain
the tides?
Why don't we share with one another how we
perceive the stories behind our eyes?
Why can't you allow me to be free as I give you the
lead?
Why can't you allow me to heal all of those painful
things?...
...from your past...
Can my "corney" jokes make you laugh?
Is there anything within you that I could grab?...
...and feel blessed to have?
If I sprayed you with a water gun, would you get
mad?
Can I dive deep down into your soul...
...and anything you're feeling inside you'll let me
know?
If I want to paint you, would you find that lame?
When I get upset, this temper, do you have the
patience to tame?
Quick to acknowledge...
...possess so much knowledge...
...yet...
As "innocent" as a child...
If I question you, will you still for a while?
Quietly shaking my head as I continue to joke and
smile
My life seems to be falsely gilded

Folks view me as astute instead of a creative person, humble, and a realist
Open my eyes?
I want to explore the skies with you and will explain the reasons why…
…hoping your eyes feel it's "magical"…
Real life yet something a bit fantastical…
…more questions than answers…
Can I be your choreographer as you be my personal dancer?
To see the beauty of the earth, can you make time?
…and will your eyes be as wide open as mine?

The Wind

The wind…
That wind…
Caresses my face as it passes around my body
Fondling me in a sense
Yet…
Giving me a sense of peace
A sense of relief
Reminding me of things we can't see…
…but can feel
I question most things and search for answers
Often feel like I'm on puppet strings, but don't want
to be the dancer?
I have an eye for beautiful things
Watching the sunrise used to make my soul sing…
The beauty thereof is undefined
A business woman with an artistic heart, soul, and
mind
Talk about confusion?...
I'm on the opposite end of Confucius
I'm the rebellious one with more thoughts than my
words could ever convey
From the smallest discolored strand of grass to the
most gorgeous nebulae
This planet is the most beautiful, and I'm firm in
what I say
I revere the sunset and sunrise
So beautiful they used to have my eyes opened wide
And at night…

…I share my plight through my thoughts, prayers, writings, and art
Often wondering why I have such an intense and deep heart
The type that will relieve you yet drown you
May not be used to a love like this, and can't "breathe", I'll resuscitate you
The wind…
That wind…
Has duel sides
It can be peaceful, endearing, relaxing…
Yet?...
…can be tragic…
…I just wanna hand you a fantasy…
…maybe a piece of magic…

<u>Vision</u>

A vision?

Yes just resting in the back of my mind: a fantasy

From the moment I laid eyes on thee: smitten

Like a story told yet unwritten

Beauty and brains for my eyes have seen the glory

Couldn't imagine anything more perfect for me

Then I awakened the next morning to sunlight

beaming on my face

That vision, that fallacy, that fantasy…erased

Like a shadow that can't be viewed in daylight

Only real to me in my dreams when I close my eyes

at night

A vision?

Yes just resting in the back of my mind: that

endearing crush

From the moment I laid eyes on thee: I knew you

were someone I could never touch…

A vision?...

She is

She is…

A conqueror, a survivor full of strength from the depths of the valley she's arisen

An aura, a definitively powerful presence with inner beauty as her weapon almost foretold like she was previously written

To be a victor although her life has been an annoying splinter, a thorn stuck in her side

And even with tears staining the back of her eyes everyone can see her pride and the fearlessness in her eyes

A level of courage undefined because she is a woman of great depth and strength

Even when knocked into a black hole she comes out practically unscathed no cuts or tears only dents

That heal, they heal, as she bows her head and kneels; like a song those wounds never last long for sure

Even when she shouts, has her doubts, and bouts of
frustration, she knows without God in life she
couldn't endure

Alone, she's never alone as long as his majesty loves
her and has her back anytime she calls

When the world attacks, and her back is up against
the wall, it is he that carries her when she falls

Our lady Yar, great woman of strength but that
strength is only defined by he who gives her the
confidence to face anything

Better things await as she open her eyes to promise
of the gates that remain open 24 hours a day cause
that's the reward faith brings

And in the rain she dances and sings because she's
made it out of the valley; she's arisen

Because she gives praise for days and believe in the
aura that was foretold and previously written

She is…

…a woman of God…

The Silhouette

Whispers of the mind, obscene yet conceiving

Visions appeasing, pleasing, maybe even self-
deceiving

The silhouette that appears in the dark

Completely stark, leaving permanent marks, by
surprise easily captures the heart

Radiance surpassing that of an exotic flower

Causes others to cower with the desire to devour

As one remembers down to the minute, every single
hour

Past yet present, attempting to evict from the mind

Very little time as we bind, and only in my dreams,
mine.

With a smile like heaven and overall beauty that's
almost surreal.

The very essence causes the unsuspecting to feel and
feel, and it's not a fallacy; the feelings are so real.

The silhouette is actually a butterfly that must spread
its wings and fly

Saying goodbye, but not goodbye

 In the mind, the silhouette cannot be denied, but on

the surface, it's easy to deny.

The desire, the flame, the yearning to replay that

game, a love that is difficult to tame yet is tamed.

As thoughts remain and feelings attempt to change,

for the silhouette with beauty as its name.

Locked in a Dream

Locked in a dream it seems

Where the world is full of beauty, love, and peaceful things

But hate abounds

As homeless people continue to wander around

People drive by with expressions of disgust

Living in a world that's difficult to trust

Feeling the pain of others as if it's your own

Wishing it was safe to let homeless people into your home.

Not turning on the television because the news is too painful

Sitting back helpless as Satan gains more souls.

A world where good people are driven cold

A world where strong people struggle not to fold.

Wishing people would love one another

Instead of stepping on and belittling each other

Reality sometimes is difficult for me to conceive.

I'd rather spend my days suspended in a dream.

I'm locked in a dream it seems

Where the world is full of beauty, love, and peaceful

things.

A place where hate cannot be found.

A place similar to how heaven sounds.

Wide Open

Wide open…

My mind and my thoughts submerged in her

Like a submarine slowly sinking to the bottom of the

ocean

So deep; with each moment I sink deeper

An unexplainable chemistry

More beautiful than a nebula

As songs play during the sunset

And trees dance rhythmically to a seemingly

inaudible tune

My mind and thoughts submerged in her

So deep; with each moment I sink deeper…

She has me wide open…

Intense

Intense…

So intense

Like lightning striking from the ground upwards

Like a gusty wind of a tsunami

Like a sunset peaking a mist a storm

So much beauty throughout chaos

A silent presence

That most don't seem to recognize for what it is

A talent that seems to be a shadow not many can see

Within the proper light

Similar to gazing unto the sky for the stars in

daylight

Unseen…

Unnoticed…

Unrecognized…

A passion so strong most don't seem to comprehend

An unimaginable strength yet a vulnerability that

remains hidden

Like a rainbow that briefly shines during a
treacherous storm

Intense…

So intense…

Like lightning striking from the ground upwards

Like the gusty wind of a tsunami

Like a sunset peaking through a storm…

Unseen…

Unnoticed…

Unrecognized…

But…

Throughout it all…

Will never be forgotten…

<u>Intrepid</u>

Intrepid; a fearlessness well known to my being

Trying to relax, but my eyes are unsure of what

they're seeing

Dove deep down into the ocean yet haven't crest the

soul

Like an iceburg, I'm seeing the surface yet so much

is unknown

Intriguing; it intrigues me

An unconscious motivation that precedes me

Unrecognizable to the conscious mind…

…yet real so real in my dreams outside of the realms

of time

Intense; yes I'm so very intense

I want to make you feel something every time we

kiss

Whether lust or love…

Have a feeling I may never have your love…

But in the meantime…

I'm intrepid; fearless in pursuing you

I should stop myself, but my soul recognizes you

Whether here or there; to or fro; I'm right where I

belong

Our souls speak a silent tune and a similar song…

In sense even in tense yet the problem is the tense

An issue with two tired hearts with different

"perceptions" at hence

Still reeling from past pain; can we heal each other?

Put a bandage on the wounds and lean on one

another?

Intrepid; a fearlessness well known to my being

I'm an Aries, my eyes recognize exactly what I'm

seeing…

…and I'm going after it…

…win, lose, or draw….

<u>Breathe</u>

Breathe…

Just breathe…

Pay attention to the sound of your heart

The rhythm has a reason

Listen…

Just listen…

To how it thumps

The rhythm has a reason

Breathe…

Just breathe…

Inhale the hidden melody

The rhythm has a reason

Listen…

Just listen…

Beats faster with every thought

The rhythm has a reason

Breathe…

Just breathe…

Stop dismissing your heart

Focus on the reason behind the rhythm…

Now just breathe…

Deeply Woven

Deeply woven…

To the point where some drown within my essence

Or dismiss it entirely…

Intense…

My intensity is as deep as the ocean

All that I am has drowned the both of us into the

depths of the Marinara

A place where light isn't supposed to exist yet I

illuminate you

And you warm the dark creases of my soul in the

coldest waters

A love that's complicated yet simple

Flowing deep into the core yet barely touches the

surface

An unpredictability that defies everything that makes

sense

An unexplainable chemistry that will never be

forgotten

But…

I must swim to the surface to allow myself to breathe

I may have been a victim of a fantasy my mind concocted

My mind is clouded like a thick fog in early spring

Been through so much not really knowing what to think

I know that I need to inhale…exhale…inhale…then exhale again

Slowly struggling to breathe as my heartbeat stops

And my mind grows numb

Deeply woven…

To the point where I've drowned myself…

In an illusion

My intensity is as deep as the ocean…

I feel like I've been drowned into the lowest depths of the Marinara…

Struggling to swim to the surface…

…so I can breathe…

I'm Me

All I can do is be me…

Nothing to prove

Nothing to hide

Just simple old me with a lot of love inside

Aimed towards a special one

I want to give her all of my love

From her hair follicles to her toe nails

From her inner being to the breath she inhales

From soothing her mind to touching her soul

From capturing her heart and never letting go

A vision that feels so real to me

Hoping I'm not deluding my mind with a fantasy

Feelings so strong I can't find the words to explain

As I wait for her, I hope her interest doesn't change

All I can do is be me…

Nothing to prove

Nothing to hide

Just simple old me with a lot of love inside

Aimed towards the woman that makes me feel so

alive…

...I love her...

Erotica; The Way You're Desired

Feeling the heat between us while staring into your
eyes

Yearning for you to feel with your lips the moisture
between my thighs

When I kiss your lips, I love it when you sign a bit

And the look in your eyes makes me yearn for you to
lick my southern lips

The blues in my thighs and the thought of you
giving my body contorted schisms

For the sexual chemistry is provoked as my body
matches your body's rhythms

We grind and grind as the sexual tensions increase

Making you hot as you place your hands on my back
digging your nails inside of me

The sighs?

The moans?

Just waiting to release a scream

As I lick up and down, I can feel your body scream

Pleased with me as I bite, kiss, blow, and suck

Your back arcs as we both become the victims of
our lust
Going in and out, on top to the bottom, as we
intensely stare into each other's eyes
Feeling the tremble of my thighs as I reach towards
the sky
The passion and emotion flowing into the depths of
the soul that I can't help myself; I'm addicted
Yearning to make you have orgasm after orgasm
every time we kick it
Feeling the heat between us while consistently
piercing your eyes
When I kiss your lips, I love it when you sigh
Yearning to feel your lips between the moisture of
my thighs
I want you to be the one to put a smile on my face
and be a blues in my thighs…

Breathlessness

Breathlessness…

When around you, I feel a sense of peace

A calming affect unfamiliar to my being has been

released

Rarely even stare at the stars at night

My "lonliness" seems to have disappeared in a sense

right before my eyes

Instead of gazing at the stars, I like to gaze at you

…because you are more beautiful than the stars

The black canvas of the night skies offer me a

surface for my mind to "paint" you from afar

And the beauty, serenity, and mystery within them is

breath-taking at times

…but not as breath-taking as you…

Seeing you today made me feel some type of way;

butterflies in my stomach like only you can do

Made me see the angels of heaven as the sky moved

the clouds

Although I want you, I don't have much to offer you

right now

But in future's tense, I could hand you the world…

Hoping one day you'll wait on me and be my girl

Breathlessness…

When around you, I feel so relieved

For the first time in my life, I'm certain that this is

where I want to be

Whether as friends, lovers, or my wife

I want and need you in my life…

<u>Ready to Love</u>

I was ready to love…

To give all of me to that special one

Although I was hesitant…

Not knowing if I had room in my heart for another

The love I had for my past was seemingly inerasable

Didn't think I was capable of letting anyone in

Although I was ready…

Confusion struck my being

Afraid to completely open my heart yet afraid to

close it

I was ready for love…

From our first conversation, from the moment we

locked eyes…

I clearly saw your soul

Behind your smile, there was pain in the back of

your eyes

My mirror; I saw my reflection every time I stared

We couldn't stop smiling at each other

And we both unlocked the diaries of our lives

Undressed our hearts

Wearing loosely held towels around our souls

I yearned for love…

Your reflection and mine were incomprehensibly

similar yet differed

Drastically…

We became deeply imbedded; prematurely

The way you looked at me…

I could feel your thoughts; I could feel the emotions

you hid

When I looked at you…

I lit a fire in you unfamiliar to your being…

That frightened yet intrigued you…

I surrendered to love…

To hear your voice, brought peace to my noisy world

To make you smile, felt like heaven

I undressed your body

You undressed my soul

When we touched, I could feel your heart

Every time we touched, I snatched a piece of your
soul

The intensity was unfamiliar…

So you ran away…

I was reproached for love…

Reeled accusations that belonged to another

My peaceful world became chaotic

Pushed further and further to the edge

Holding on tightly in an attempt to prove myself

But with each tear…

My heart grew colder and colder

As you snatched the towel from around my soul

And smacked me with it

I was ready to love…

I was ready for love…

I yearned for love…

I surrendered to love…

I was reproached for love…

My heart ached to love…

My heart ached for love…

My heart ached…

I was ready for love…

But you weren't

You undressed and shattered my soul…

I've never felt so naked

But now…

I'm fully clothed

And afraid to undress…

<u>My Imagination</u>

Silence…
Breathlessness as I envision you…
My mind wondering into so many different realms
Never met you yet secretly yearn for you
Is this my mind playing tricks on me again?
A mirage that I've seen since childhood
A silhouette without a face or a name
Unconsciously recognizing the attributes
Smitten in a sense
Two souls speaking to each other on
incomprehensible levels
Yet…
We haven't even met
Is this just my imagination?
Or…
Do you actually exist?
A joyful fallacy within a false reality
Or…
Am I simply a hopeless romantic in love with the
fact of being in love?
Shhhh!
I need to quiet my mind and tame this heart
So open…
So honest…
Too strong and real for the faint hearted
Never learns her lesson for she's open 24 hours a
day
Incapable of closing…
Refuses to shut down or build walls…

Nothing is greater than love…
And much love is what is given yet not readily
received…
My soul speaks in variety of languages…
But only a few vibes with the rhythms
My heart sends out vibrations not many understand
It is just my imagination?
The inclination of you and me one day?
Silence…
Breathlessness as I envision you…
A victim of my imagination…
Perhaps…
Hopelessly devoted to a mirage…

<u>Sigh</u>

Sigh...
Louder than a whisper yet communicates so much
Vague yet understood; a sound as powerful as a
touch
Often comes out when words can't express
Thoughts and feelings someone's demure has
caressed
Unrestrained; expelled unpredictably
Whose meaning is understood subconsciously
You just know, you just know; an automatic
translation
A simple sound that's its very own conversation
Vague yet understood; a sound as powerful as a
touch
Louder than a whisper yet communicates so much
Sigh...

Like A Whisper

Every thought is like a whisper; imagining the
warmth of your breath massaging my ear
Remembering the soft touch of your skin as my
fingers slipped between yours; an electrifying
sensation that provoked a little fear
An intense stare that has me envisioning our souls
intertwined as one in a forbidden dance
Floating on the same vibration; a frequency of
intensive passion unto the spiritual as our bodies are
in a sacred trance
To give and receive, to give and receive; building the
foundation for a lifetime of prosperity as we engage
in a love unlike another
Wanting to explore your mind, caress your heart,
and whisper a language to your soul like a melody
specifically played for one another
The sound of your voice echoes, it echoes, it echoes;
vibrating my rhyme and rhythm like a blues in your
thighs
Wanting to make your body explode like contorted
schisms; breathlessness as satisfaction is reflected in
your eyes
To kiss, to bite, to scratch, to embrace, to love every
inch of your physical being
You're more addictive than crack; tunnel vision - no
one but you is what I'm seeing
Like a CD that skips saying the same thing thrice
You tore down my walls the moment you entered
my life

Every thought is like a whisper; imagining the warmth of your breath massaging my ear
Remembering the soft touch of your skin as my fingers slipped between yours; an electrifying sensation that made everything clear...
...it's you, and only you, I want to behold...
...I want you; mind, body, heart, and soul...

Silence

Silence...
Hollowed; a sacred cross not well esteemed
Dismayed by thoughts that are louder than screams
Unconscious motivations not quite understood
Internal wars of the tyranny of the shoulds
Breathlessness as those awaiting to exhale
Being sold without profiting from the sale
Silent cries as a means for the soul to scream
Words left unspoken; feigned emotions left to be
seen
Silence...
Your silence rings in my soul louder than any scream
Wounds deep into the spirit hidden behind the
scenes...
Concealed by a feigned smile...

No One's Left

There's a rain cloud over my head storming over me
Even on sunny days without a cloud in the sky that
cloud is hovering over me
Not fully comprehending how the ending could be
so hearttrending
All I have left are the memories of our beginnings,
in-betweens, and the way I felt at your ending
This leaves me confused, so soon, because I am
already missing you
At times, I feel I am losing my mind; praying to God
to tell me what I am to do
No response, so I sit up for days as my tears spray
I'm so tired, so tired because I haven't slept; I
haven't slept
In a crowded room, I feel there's no one left

As the sun rises, I tell myself that I will be strong
My plan is to begin my day off right, but without you
everything seems so wrong
I call off work because I can't focus
Don't want to eat, because when I do, I feel like I'm
choking
When alone, I speak aloud hoping you can hear the
words spoken
Your love is like a song that plays on repeat in my
soul
I sit up for days, because even though I have to, I
am not ready to let you go
I'm so tired, I'm so tired because I haven't slept; I

haven't slept
In a crowded room, I feel there's no one left

There's no more tears, but I am frustrated, confused,
hurt, sick, and sad
I'm tired of being tired of feeling this way, so it
eventually makes me mad
Emotions imploding, eroding the positive thoughts
that my heart so desperately requests
For the first time in my life, I admit, I feel more
cursed than blessed
At this moment, God touched my shoulder and said,
"My child, why are you so stressed?"
I stared at God and answered, "Lord, I'm so tired. I
am so tired. I haven't slept. I haven't slept. In a
crowded room, I feel there's no one left."
God replied, "Don't feel alone because you are never
alone. My child, no one left because I called them
home."

Damaged

I am an open book yet a mystery
I am easy to talk to, but it's difficult to get close to
me
My eyes tell all; there's nothing I can hide
But my demeanor fools most; they never know what
I'm feeling inside
I am a positive person who is sometimes too strong
for her own good
I have a love/hate relationship with being
misunderstood
I have a heart of gold and my depth of caring runs
so deep
Thoughts and ideals run through me constantly
keeping me from a good night's sleep
A "strange" sista that awakens in the middle of the
night to paint her dreams
My silence is sometimes silence, but at other times,
it's my scream
I'm not a "bad" person just uniquely me
Sometimes I feel "society" has me bound by chains
and I just want to break free
Who am I?
People often resort to trying to figure me out
But they always fall short without a doubt
To get to know me, just look deeply into my eyes
No emotion I can hide, and if I trust you, I will let
you inside.

Like A Breeze

A breeze...
Like a summer's passing through the hollows of time
Whispering ambiguities as intangible as a reason
The heat of the flame feeling twice removed
Surrendered...
It surrendered; we surrendered...
The fantasy for a veracity too unfeigned for the
imagined
Fluid; like sounds heard when submerged
underwater
Gasping for air although we're already above the
surface
Once ignited flames within from a simple glance
Torching the sheets with our rhymes and rhythms
Inexplicable how the storm clouds emerged
Removing the heat and dousing the flame
Burned out; it burnt out...
Leaving smoldering coals willing to reignite in
present or future tense
The winter never felt colder
Remembering the summer before its passing
The air was so crisp to inhale
The warmth from the sun penetrated my essence
Sigh; I sighed...
My heart skipped a beat as my soul smiled
Whispering ambiguities as intangible as a song
Like a winter's passing through the hollows of time
The breeze?...
...I still feel it...

Art is Beauty

When I look at the sunrise, I see beauty, hope, and a
new beginning
When I look at the sunset, I see beauty, completion,
and God's footprints across the sky like an abstract
painting
When I gaze at the stars, I see mystery, possibility,
and so much beauty it boggles my mind; they look
like gemstones sprinkled against a black canvas
When I watch water rushing down a creek, I hear a
beautiful orchestra and see the meaning of life
When I see branches blowing, I see dancers moving
to the beat of the wind
When I see a flower, I see a beautiful, fragile
sculpture
Beauty surrounds me
When I see...
I see deeply...
Because I see...
Art everywhere...